A LITTLE
Life

POETRY SUFFICES

SUSAN MARSHALL

Copyright © 2023 Susan Marshall
All Rights Reserved

Year of the Book
135 Glen Avenue
Glen Rock, PA 17327

ISBN: 978-1-64649-381-4 (paperback)
ISBN: 978-1-64649-382-1 (ebook)

This book or parts thereof may not be reproduced in any form, stored in any retrieval system, or transmitted in any form by any means—electronic, mechanical, photocopy, recording, or otherwise—without prior written permission of the publisher, except as provided by United States of America copyright law.

The following poems have previously appeared in *Reflections* magazine, Notre Dame of Maryland University:

- A Valentine to My Mother
- After Easter
- Anniversary
- As We Move into Fall
- Beer Locker in Tornado Alley
- Challenge
- Diagnosis
  as "Diagnosis Is Destiny"
- Elysium
- In the Deep Woods
- Invitation
- Loch Raven
- Making of the Poet
- Meditation
- Notes
- Sea Wind Musings
- Rerun 2020
  as "Sonnet for 2020"
- September 11, 2015
  as "9/11/2015"
- Summer's Scheme
  as "As She Must"
- Teacher
- Tanka
  as "as the season ripens"
- The Poetry Changes
- What Do You Do
  with the Blues?

Cover image: Tracy Marshall, Forest Lawn Cemetery, Fredonia, NY

In memory of

Sister Maura Eichner, SSND,
who told me I would write
when I was ready.

Isaac Rehert,
whose encouragement
made this book possible.

Contents

Forest Lawn 1
On Poetry 3
A Few Greeks 15
The Presence of Absence 23
Cycles 37
Copper Pennies 43
Months 51
Wanderings and Wonderings 67
H_2O 85
Family 95
Progression 109
Currents 119
War 131
Music 145
My Yard 155
Pen to Paper 167
Closing Lines 179
One Absolutely Last Poem 187

FOREST LAWN
FREDONIA, NEW YORK

Slant-light of the cemetery sun
slivers the evening shade
spotlights both marble and worn
to wordlessness stone
our ancestors' graves
still, scattered among their companions
a company of aged trees
a play of grazing deer
awaiting us as they do year to year

ON POETRY

Lessons from the Poets

With regards to Robert Bly, W.S.
Merwin, Stanley Kunitz

First, cut off the top of your head.
(But leave your ears to judge what they think right.)
Then dive deep, freely, if in fear, lest
mere depression charge too dear a toll
for you to reach the bottom of your soul,
to sail it through the race's DNA,
(alive in you) where some word or image
waits to grab your pen. Dream it true.
Senses in flight, the lonely day and night
are all that you can know of what you write.
But you, the unambitious chronicler
of life, unfolds the ancient into the careless
Now. Poetry sings salvation to the land.
Someone may read, someone may understand.

I Have Read the Great Poets

Revise a poem tens of times
before they consider it done
Is that troublesome comma
that may consume an afternoon
worthy of account

I have seen revisions
in which the final bore no resemblance
to version number one

For Keats, *Heart aches* and *My heart aches*
vie for first line until *My heart aches*
wins and can dissolve with him
into that winged song eternal
of which it is said he writes
in the morning sun of a day in May
then puts the poem away

ON READING KEATS' *WHEN I HAVE FEARS THAT I MAY CEASE TO BE*

The days tilt down
the numbered years rise
to a point, a logical spot
where they could stop
without surprise

No fatal illness, just life
to urge my incomplete
scattered contemplation
of that shore

Where Keats stands
thinking

I have not an unlived youth
a budding love, a passionate
waiting pen, nor fame
to lose, but a too quiet age

Yet would I stand on that wintry edge
thinking
into readiness before I slip off
easy and curious

A LITTLE LIFE
thoughts on Emily Dickinson

There must have been some
quiet amidst the high humor
the sibling love and play and learning
despite the singing garden
and the housework
Quiet enough to build a hidden trove
of poems

Then the dying
the to-do of discovery
excitement when the judgers
found the poems good
enough — and "fixed" them
then knew to fix them back
The noise of the press
the clamor of praise

Now all those souls still —
still and eternally
quiet as black marks
on a silent page

MAKING OF THE POET

His mother had a hard time staying dead.
Her starring *Juliet* a nightly role
he learned by heart, until the tell-tale red
with cough forever closed her eyes of coal.

This pallid dark-eyed loss repeated thrice.
All women loved succumbed to crimson gore,
while poverty and genius rolled the dice
and tossed him to the streets of Baltimore.

Old Dickens once had told him, through his tears,
of his lost pet, his raven, who sipped paint;
mistake that killed and lives in listeners' ears
from that first knocking, threatening and faint.

The sun never warmed his own short story.
It burns now, despite the grave, in glory.

INVITATION

A nod to Billy Collins

You have to ease into having nothing
to write, relax into confrontation
with the empty paper needing lines
the mirroring space inside your head
because everything is too big to fit
into a poem or is too small to fit
into a poem
So, you read

This poet can fill a stanza, a page
and a half, on memory of his last
cigarette, an icy day, a trip not
taken, a circle of salt on the table
where he sits
with nothing particular
to say

Poetry

I sit down in melancholy
mood suitable to suffering
along with the poets.
I turn not to Mary Oliver's advice on letting go,
but to Keats, to his fear of letting go,
till peering over that edge,
in thought, swallows even his fears.
Then to Shakespeare's warning
to his love to lose his name
when he is gone, for gone
he will be — as will we.
But suddenly, Billy Collins is slowly,
laboriously undressing Emily
Dickenson and feathery hope
wafts me to his neighbor's famous
barking dog
who still performs unending
arias to Beethoven's symphonies
because the happy poet is lucky enough
to be unarmed.

Notes from the Side Porch of My B&B Across the Street from Emily Dickinson's House

Because I look through leaves to her corner
bedroom window where she wrote
at her tiny sun-splashed desk, I am compelled
to write. Because if her spirit roams
she might be pleased. I avoid dashes
and surprising caps lest she bemoan.

The floor is worn beside her bed, between
her windows, where she paced her thoughts
into poems.

Because Main Street is no longer a dirt road
but a paved ribbon of traffic and sirens and
modernity
pedestrians do not look up to glimpse
a shadow at the glass.
She would be pleased.

Because I left my only pencil on her grave
I scribble in pen. Among papers, flowers, stones
someone left her a pair of black heels.

At her house I see a robin chase
a moth through the air
and lose it. He stands a second on her grass
to look at me and he eats nothing raw.

I could make of him a thing of great personal
significance.

A long list, this, and I want
only to compose a few good lines
about magic and the woman
who looked out the window and saw
Everything.

I had met a couple at breakfast,
headed home to Poughkeepsie,
suggested they go across the street
first. Why else be here?

We all take the two hour tour.
The wife thanks me repeatedly
then heads home to discover
The Poetry
I have helped change the world.

Mary Oliver Has Died

*"By morning I had vanished at least a dozen times
into something better."*
—Mary Oliver, Sleeping in the Forest

At first I took the news as one must
take the news these days,
with a shake of the head at one more assault
on reason and the senses.
But I have had time.
I return to her work and I ask,
Who now will remind us that we *are* nature,
as surely as dog, deer, flower or bug?
So fully does she live this truth in her poetry
that she sets some critics on edge —
men skittish in their praise
of such deep feminine experience.

Her forest burns, her wild geese fly, her owl hunts
and our mortal requirements are illuminated.

I have been told that Oliver is too didactic.
But I say she had so little time,
just one life,
to recall us to our home,
to our dying, and to our being.

A FEW GREEKS

Agamemnon

For a long time my favorite word,
all those soft vowels, smooth consonants,
nothing to bring you up short
like a sudden *take* or *slake* or *fake*
but all smooth and as pleasing as *father*.
Agamemnon just slips through your lips
and, of course, as king, leader of the Greeks
at Troy when you first encounter the actor
in his own play, he impresses.
Is he not your protagonist?

But life is full of disillusionment.
That smooth fellow can lose his magic
as you learn discernment,
his choices not so endearing.
If you must slay your daughter
to get to war, you might do it
with less enthusiasm
and come home to her mother,
enslaved princess in tow,
more bathed in penitence.

So there I am, caught in a dilemma.

Agamemnon has lost some shine
but is still easier to say
than Clytemnestra,
wife and mother and avenger,
who seems to want you to think
as you speak
her name.

MYCENAE, 1988

Men hawk huge oranges to quench the thirst
— blown in on the hot, blue wind —
in the parking lot, where armies
of tourists are discharged.

The roaring silence of the Lions' Gate swallows
the words of the guides, the chatter of sightseers.
Below, the slippery, sun-smoothed stones
point to glaring excavations of round royal tombs.

Inside the gate the wind-worn stones pave
the ascent to the upper chambers,
become, for me, the floor of the queen's bedroom,
the bath, where one hollyhock rises through stone.

Uncaged for the day, and unheeded,
school children run and shout,
make weather-rounded stones stained
and slippery with spilled juice.

Still, the ancient wailing silence overwhelms
sound and the hot wind carries the children's
laughter into time, and into the neighboring hills
Greeks call The Sleeping Agamemnon.

CASSANDRA

Always the betrayal at the start,
the fall of the kingly house
and the promises broken. Sybil's
voice stolen by a usurping god and given
to the girl with certain angry stipulations.
Her voice denied, silenced into careful
observation for self-preservation,
but silence cannot hold.
The girl's world grows
and she is called to witness,
becoming one of the unheard
chorus, dismissed
under humanity's hot sun,
almost wishing to be among the deaf
and careless as all are hurried
on their way to meet the queen.

Medea Muses in Athens

That I killed him
I doubt. His sonless heart
in silence beats its coded rhythm
to the stars
who flash a silent response.
Alone, a worm I have made
of this *once* man.
And I, of the sun born
have given him his just night.
I am of the sun.
I pace this alien place,
exiled exile
I cannot see through the dark.
I am night.

Elysium

When the tragedian Euripides died
old Sophocles bade his own actors
wear mourning onstage
This, the year before
he too at last was happy

THE PRESENCE OF ABSENCE

PROFESSOR

For Jo Trueschler

We should all die of heartbreak
she says, simply because
life dares ask for itself
something worth missing

She says it simply because
the spring sun smiles on us
Something worth missing
so near and so far

The spring sun smiles on us
as we read together a tale of loss
so near and so far
we could all die of heartbreak

NOAH THE OAK TREE

For Mary Oliver

No doubt grows still
in family, rooted, serene.
Has he had time to notice,
each first day of spring,
that she no longer comes to hug
his girth, to kiss him—
the one who passed one day
on all fours so that she could see
as the fox sees?

Is her absence a presence itself,
rooted and silent and sure as the oak
in this her chosen world?

For her breath fed the trees,
her prayer was her witness
of the lives of things here,
of her old friend Noah.

Challenge

Nearly two years since Tucker died.
Staunch spirit flown.
One needled yelp
delivering

freedom and taking love and pain
bound each together
in one old dog
looking to me

in trust. Three dogs gone. And time.
Dare we tempt old hearts?
Dare we puppy
our lives again?

TREE HUGGER

I have hugged trees
in self-conscious joy
to test the depth of satisfaction
in living that derogatory phrase.
Those trees did not sigh, protest or laugh,
though they are so much slower than we
they may still be forming their responses.

We now know trees converse, share food,
execute emergency plans,
but cannot flee the saw,
the shredder and the axe.

We hear their lamentation for the lost
among them only in the wind,
our ear so dull.

The air that fills that newly empty space
where once stood grandeur
cannot hold the sparrow, the squirrel,
or our eye,
cannot fill our open arms,
holds only the ghost of the tree.
And only for those who knew it.

TOWARD SLEEP

Is the movement of November
Trees undress for their rest
Night falls heavy
Clouds blanket
But the chill holds

It seems a frightening time
To die
No hopeful rose-colored sky
No choir of birds
No butterfly to distract
Mourners and feed
Their need to believe
Just dank cold
And the smell of coffee
In an empty house

Teacher

For Margaret Doyle

I have sat by this window many other springs
seeking in the white blossoms, suddenly greened
trees, and deepening sky, inspiration
for yet another poem of inevitable praise.

Today I attend a memorial for my friend and mentor,
a poet who gazed thinkingly at so many spring
miracles, so many seasonal reasons to write.

Are you enough sated with dogwoods and daffodils,
Margaret, to travel eternity and never be emptied?

What Do You Do with the Blues?

He says,
after spilling his grief
in hoarse, whispery voice —
when emotion turns,
as it must momentarily do,
to humor and to hope —
"Well, at least we know
she'll be redecorating."

"You bet," I say,
uneasy, just a little,
that she might have to go
with blues and whites
up there
and, like mine, her palette
runs to reds and greens and
earth tones.

You just can't live with blues
when you are at home
in the reds and the greens
and the earth tones.

Funny how that idea,
that potential little problem,
has stayed with me
through these past days.

DISTANCES

We live but a few blocks apart
amid empty promises to meet
as our years fall away. Take heart.
We live. But a few blocks apart
her doctors are hoping she'll start
to have days she's happy to greet.
We live but a few. Blocks apart.
Amid empty promises, we meet.

An Accounting

She held firmly though loosely
that thread of friendship
for over forty years
It was she who called me so long ago
after she became ill
who arranged to meet
who said I was her first sister
of the heart as she was merely
brothered by blood
who included me in her premature
farewell tour

Then it was for me to call her
to keep in touch to keep
pace with the progress of disease
to absorb this nurse's analysis
dissection of odds and symptoms
and time
to talk of ordinary things
It was for me to praise
helplessly from afar
her courage to fight
for the right to die

Then it was I who held our thread
too loosely
days and days behind its final dropping

I Lost Another Friend
This Week

The losing becomes less and less
unusual, the surprise smaller
or at least brief — at this age.
The regret curls into wonder
that that woman — that face, voice, energy
was indeed mortal, though I knew.
I guess at what she now knows
if she now knows.

I have seen my peers mourn
peers together, almost never
do they weep. We speak quietly.

Alone, I gaze into the day, find
myself nodding, as if to answer,
"Yes"

POETRY SUFFICES

I send my sister Billy Collins
collections because she is
now in need of poetry
and a stranger to it
her dying friend in need
of reason to smile
They will find more in the poems,
I think, than humor

Too late
That sleep wins out
Consciousness
comes in such brief snaps

CYCLES

Summer's Scheme

She came cool in her dress and promising
heat. Like her sisters, now spent, anticipated in joy,
for she delights our carefree desires with her
jeweled berries, sweet greens, yellows and golds,
her fairy pinks, flaming reds from ordered
plots and untamed gardens, and the wild flash
of firefly in the sheltering wood.
She wears, it seems, mysterious timelessness
though she smiles and sheds, in stealth, that
gossamer illusion, and at last we mourn
her approaching death, even as she gathers
her harvest; the late ripening fruit, as in the darkest
storms of the season, she has harvested human
song and beauty and heart, even as she must.

As We Move into Fall

We clear away what we do not need
faint memories
things of summer
As we move into fall
we consider our next move
unsought but lurking
We calmly discuss if and when
because we are merely moving into fall
because it is not yet winter

BALMY IN BALTIMORE
JANUARY 2012

Summery weightless moods
greening with the woodland trails
Smiling like a sun-sillied frog
circling the current
in the pot on the fire

Dogwoods Are Abloom

Outside my window the tops
of the dogwood boughs are playing
in the April wind.
These blossoms have come, as always,
and they will fade and fall like dusky
dirty snow.
Yet in their few weeks they offer
bright white significance,
it seems, into our lives.
Spring's energetic surprise
quickens the blood into expectation.

But always there are those who suffer
simultaneously with this self-confident show.
Do they breathe in the scented promise
and believe? Do the trees' petals sway
the worried heart, hold in light
the fading eye?
Or does this bridal white
merely mock in its indifference
as it is indifferent to both day and night?

COPPER PENNIES

ON EVOLUTION

Beauty saves us or slays us, I learn
Does vanity beget vanity
that uncoils the upward spiral
or does beauty beget beauty
that strengthens it?

We love images of our DNA's birthplace —
Savannahs' grassland dotted with trees
we once climbed for safety —
our innate memory

Today we may trace our own ancestry
back a few hundred years
to names without faces
— those who are responsible for us —
and realize the miracle of continuity
despite the missing and the lost

We carry the beautiful blood forward
ignorant of the end
even our meager comprehension
a dangerous and a lovely thing

SHE SAID:

If today I should miss the train, ask
that it wait at Noonan's Island,
and you will hear the sound of my feet
following along the woven steel
that spans the water,
deep and swift below.

For we two have clung to our appointed
track, wheeling ever over the waiting,
rutted, flattened path of our little
destinies honed, movement zoned,
and we not asked before set upon
our measured, silent, parallel
rack, where we want to go.

Photo of a Boy

He looks out to the water
to the mystery from which
he has come
Just past toddlerhood
hands in back pockets, shirt and jeans
waiting for him to grow into them
his hair all sun
and we see, now that we know,
with eyes that seek the man he will be
We cannot have patience for all the needed
days and weeks and years

Better perhaps to leave him
in his reverie, to hold him
in ours, this small living
being whose tomorrow is as sure
as our own

THE ERRAND

Venture, then, in youth,
into beautiful unknowns
bearing your little basket
of gifts barely nurtured,
barely one nutritional meal,
lacking seasoning.

Caped in innocence, think
to feed your world. Traipse
through the sunny meadows
and through the forests,
of shelter or of defeat,
accommodating both
the cooling shade
and the calculating wolf
in its den of disguises,
glowing, perhaps, like the
open arms of your journey's
end; the restful lap,
rewarding embrace
of your mothers' mothers.

When you look into the eyes
of the wolf, will you see
yourself, savior or devourer
of your own dreams?

IF I HAD A PILE OF COPPER PENNIES

As deep as fallen leaves and as bright
in the light, mix of golden reds
to dreary browns
years etched upon them
some dark with age or troubled days
some shining still as if newly minted
or softly saved
I might find a match for each year
I've raked into my store, the compost
and coin through which I live today

MONTHS

January

I am trying to emulate my peers —
to downsize, to let go —
a box of books, a pan or two,
my husband's knee-worn jeans.
None of the *old* holiday decorations
recently removed and repacked
have left the area.
This started with a gift — a 40-piece dinnerware set
meant to replace my *suddenly beloved* old,
mismatched, chipped and cracked pieces.
I did pitch the worst, tried
to send the best off to be sold
but could not.
They remain.
One of the new salad plates arrived broken.
The store replaced it with another 40-piece set.
They do not want it back.
So, in the new year cleansing scheme, I am rid
a box of books, if I take it away, a pot or two,
jeans, not mine, and a few dishes.
Because of the 79 new ones etc. etc.
I cannot yet call my plan a success.

A Valentine to My Mother

This greeting comes late, but no matter
You've been gone so long
a convenient blank slate
I have kept mostly so
as if waiting — my lifetime —
for the colors
I seem a stickler for facts
I did color you more whitish
than black in your leaving
and in the path you took
to your early grave

I never could paint
your second wifedom
your daughter
your widowhood

I have been so passive
and she passive too — till now
this sister you bore me
bred into sadness and solitude
a witness to your own
and to the drink with which you eased
the dark and eased into that grave

The beautiful blank slate
slowly coloring in
some lights, more darks
warmed like a shot of whiskey
with the gold-red light
of the artist's desire
to paint me your life with care
as you are becoming mine

February

The sneakily warm sun
sparks fleeting thoughts of Shelley
on an Italian lake
as I walk my city street
to the post office
where I will mail,
on deadline day,
my manuscript of five poems
meant to gain me admittance
into a class of
"practiced writers"
of verse.

Absurd pretension for one who feels
quite past seeing glory in the flower
feels mostly museless
and caught up
in things of common day.

Back home, I open a volume of
Billy Collins' poems in hope
of hope and read:
loose pages of Shelley float in the air.

BASEBALL

Finally, finally, Opening Day!
Who wins, who loses
the game no matter. In weather
colder than October's close
or bright with April's fey
promise, the announcer's calls,
the crack of ball meeting
bat and you're back —

at your father's knee
learning the rules,
or riding your bike
past the radio's blare,
painting a room, soothing
a child, cooking, swimming
to home runs and outs.
All yesterday's summers
meet in today and tomorrow
is sunny and warm.

My Lost Poem

I wrote a poem about Easter once
about how the eerie clouds grazed dark
and low over our Pennsylvania hill town —
as they should — on Good Friday
How I half wanted solitude on Easter Weekend
so that I could mull that sacrificial mystery
I might have traced my journey
toward doubt in that death's seemingly
thankless job of opening heavenly gates

I might have noted those other Spring-time
Gods — Dionysius, Osiris, Inanna, who made that
three-day visit to hell

The magic about our Man on his cross
is that he loved indiscriminately and taught that
He upset the status quo
He upset the plan
Reason enough for our cross and its Man
I have not found that poem again

After Easter

The white cloth loops gracefully
along the wooden arms of the cross
in front of the church.
It is quiet, deserted, the only movement,
the cotton-polyester piece itself
as the breeze moves through it.

She is not a child, not of that sympathetic
stature, but old, enough to merit some
slight regard in her crumbly shoes,
her stretched socks, her crooked
skirt and ancient jacket which all appear
brown, no matter their real colors. Her hair
might be grey. She glances up as she totters
past the decorated cross, looks down,
continues along five sidewalk squares,
returns, stops, straightens up into study
of this symbol of departure, of release.
She steps close, reaches, removes
the white drape, adjusts it lumpily
over one shoulder as she wanders away.

PASTORAL FOR JUNE

The birds are fighting.
Two robins—symbols of spring
and innocence—shock me
with their mutual hostility
into shooing them away
from my little vegetable plot.
They fly jaggedly,
each diving into the other for one
last blow.

As I start to rake nearby, I notice
a robin's egg lying blue on the ground.
I work, circling slowly closer
as my mind circles the possibility
and problem of an unborn bird
needing its nest. Finally
I nudge the egg gently, find it
broken and empty.

My fighting robins; distraught
parents, one chiding the other's
carelessness? One, a thief, a kidnapper?
Irritable empty nesters?
Or ignorant, both, of the blue
oval emptiness quiet
at the foot of the tree?

Promises

Baltimore, July 4, 1991

Huddled in the crowd
pressed against massive
glass storefronts upscaling
the harbor,

music — stirring, loud
times the blasting flashes

Shiveringly

seeking America
in the red and blue and white
and in the gold
in the gold
in gold.

Halloween

Today's the day, tonight's the night
the princesses and pirates slight
will come for treats while it's still light.
But as this night grows dark and deep
and little ones are put to sleep
come big kids with their pillowcases
open under painted faces,
business-like and looking glum.
I wonder if they're having fun.

Soon they'll be the parents teaching
the high art of trick or treating,
then home alone to watch the door
as old earth circles round once more.

BIRTHSTONE

November, if not the cruelest month,
moves us not to odes, haiku and sonnets.
It's closing up, shutting down and fading light,
retirement-like, anticipate the white
and metaphors of ice. Poor cousin
to blooming spring's emerald life eternal,
summer's ruby reproductive passion
reaped in sapphire splendored fall, its own
allotted jewel the lukewarm, quiet
and amber hued not quite so precious stone,
for which a galumphing, sloppily loving
one-eyed St. Bernard I know was named,
is the modest, yet good enough Topaz.
Who needs April, diamonds and all that jazz?

Turkey Necks

One comes in a bag with particular
other organs, all neatly packed inside
its owners carved out cavity, said owner
being Thanksgiving Dinner. We remove
these necks and organs and boil them for broth
and to have chunks of stuff to feed the dog.
We are fairly grateful for such turkey necks.
Some turkey necks we are wearing, and we hope
they are not bagged, etc. etc. We would like
to give them to our younger friends and return
to our previous necks. Perhaps we would actually
buy lovely neck jewelry again. Yet we can be grateful
for the money we are saving and for turtlenecks.
These turkey necks remind us that we are not
our younger friends, nor anyone young, really.
Yet, we can be thankful that we still have our necks
and various other organs, more or less
where they ought to be.

ON SEASONAL SUSTENANCE

In the absence of the summer sun,
the winter one taunts us merely,
flitting and flirting with our up-
turned faces, distanced
and dozing behind blizzardy
clouds, vacationing
somewhere like Brazil
for long stretches
when only a slightly more
discernable light tells us
when it is no longer night.

But sometimes after storms,
and sometimes to surprise an
unremarkable day, it coldly
burns off the haze, reminding
us that still the sky is blue
though its edges meet not
the blossoms' red or gold,
or leaves of green, but barren
browns or the dazzling,
blinding brightness
of the snow.

WANDERINGS AND WONDERINGS

Every Day a Lot Happens

Birthing and dying—
cells to universes—and our little
wanderings and wonderings

I have often faced the blank page
with a blank mind until, in time,
a strange unbidden line has
scrawled its path against the paper,
a sliding, skittering landing
of a piece of all that happening
It rests quietly, surprised perhaps
to find itself there, a gift I may nurture,
rarely refuse

Where might it have flown
if not tipped unsuspectingly
to me?

AD: SPRING DRESSES FOR OLDER WOMEN

Well, there ought to be some assets in growing old
so if Spring wants to put on her fashion show for me,
I will attend. I will applaud, I will smile at her grace,
imagine the daffodil, crocus, dizzying hyacinth have slept
the winter through in expectation of my gaze.
A miracle of intent.
Spring bloomed for youth when I was young, the waking
into life, the quickened blood. Later the fragile sun-warmed bud
echoed the fragile new life I held in my arms.

Always, Spring has clothed herself in her luscious gowns.
We are free to admire, though free things are often undervalued.
Yet, the old come to love free offers and Spring
is a most precious and elusive bauble
toward which we hold out our hands,
reach for pink and white of the dogwood's skirt, the singing air
as the late petal falls toward summer in its last goodbye.

Haiku

yesterday's snow
is today's sunny sidewalk
teenage girls lounge

nostalgic day trip
to old camping grounds
stink bugs

growing
paper mountain
New York Times

A Moment

Even the dog is lazy
this hot spring Sunday,
sleeping or pacing, no
chew toy satisfactory, no
sidewalk traffic worth the bark.
She stops to watch the closet
door rattle with the A/C
vibrations behind it,
to look at herself in the glass
doors of the bookcase,
to look at me doing nothing
but reading Billy Collins.
She jumps back onto the bed
and closes her eyes.

I wonder how this poem
would feel had I not noted
that it is Sunday.

Dust Balls

Little miracles
reborn ever
out of the invisible

Give thanks for fertility
of the barren floor

Dance in sudden escape
from gravity
lifted by breeze
of broom or passing foot

Feed on yourself
grow free in size and shape

Airy weightless
sprites of insistent
immortality

Scuba Diving

It's not the pressure.
I have known that all along.
Pressure to be, to do.
On land I'm good. And fish. I like
fish. I caught one once and cried.
I like the scurrying minnows who sweep
a path for my plodding feet in their silty wet world.
I have seen the circling aquarium swordfish and
    companions,
worried about their glass wall breaking,
all finny things washing out with the water
as I saw in a movie once.
I think a piano was involved.
I have wondered how it is to drown in air.
I have seen the whale race our boat from afar.
I have read of one big fish or another staring down
its human nemesis at the end of a line.
I'd like to float through clear island waters,
shadowing the sand, to rest in a nook of coral, join
a colorful school basking in the water-drenched
rays of the sun. Yet I cannot dispel
this Great White Fear that lets me sink into the sea
only up to my knees.

Beer Locker in Tornado Alley

One by one or by twos and threes
they appear
young, old, sweethearts and strangers
together now on this day

The store's part-timer speeds them
into that cold storage space
gathered up like useful
odds and ends

Then all goes dark
Their dread merited
the approaching roar
the threatening void

And into this black noise
they yell indiscriminately
to one another
"I love you"

WITCHY WOMAN

Surprised by late winter's warm morning light
I notice a woman walk down the street
Image I map with interior sight

Beckoning spring in shorts, sandaled feet
Tall, thin, long hair loosed down her back, and grey
Why settled here in suburban retreat?

She belongs to another place and day
Her tie-dyes and beads contrast her lined face
with their echo of youth, of time that won't stay

with that glorious moment, too finite grace
I see that she danced, smoked, laughed in her fate
Now face down she walks her lone quiet space

I want her prime back, and mine, but it's late
Yesterday's history mocks while we wait

Moving On

Our neighborhood roads have been
repaired, made smooth. Cars
whir when they pass — unless
they need to flaunt their gears
or express their age

in pride or complaint.
Under the hood the late
models are sleek
unencumbered with all

the lines and gadgets
that attach the oily old
engines and batteries

and seemingly extraneous stuff
that keep them going. The new
are more like the antique —
simple
but oh so connected
they can barely get lost
whether they want to or not.

Death of a Bee

A bee, member of a declining race,
joins us for lunch in late October sun
Unasked, he examines the calm contours
of my companion's face, her hair, her blouse of black
barely mindful of our waving arms
the sun so warm and welcoming and lazy

He settles of a sudden on my salad
engendering in me a sudden rise from the table
Then bravely I sit and watch him climb
the sweetened dips and valleys of my lettuce
My attempt to brush him away merely lands him
under a leaf
Now coated in raspberry vinaigrette
he slides onto the slatted table

where my friend, too fast, nails him with our
McCormick Peppermill
I lift it once to find his body, slightly squirming
beneath crushed wings
I eye the now ominous weapon as we eat and chat,
bemoan to myself the wonted cruelties of this world

IF THE MOON HAPPENED ONCE

Would there be time in one brief night
for all the love and hate and war to be lit?
For those the dark is also fit.

Sold to every mortal eye
the one-time offer, as is, made and paid
with suitable gasped surprise.

Heaven's one time audition,
flood lights illuminating
just one tide

just once, the creatures of prey.
In night white gardens

the once shadowed rabbit
exposed without
practice.

Radio/Covid

First, a soft guitar, hollow as time
carries gentle vocals. *I will stay if you want me to,
I will go if you want me to,* and I hear my sunny dream
notes of the '70s, the yearning to live in the music's air.
Next, a lively choir bursts a preacher into his sermon,
Deny the historical Jesus and deny your own intelligence. I
turn to the Blues crying *The devil is on your back,* jump to
Your white, bright smile, which in a single turn becomes
Rocket your Mortgage, enhance your future—
followed, of course, by *I see an island in the Mediterranean,*
and only one station is warning us to stay home.
Cycle complete, I return to NPR where a monologue
skit of a woman trying to connect to another human
in a train station works for laughs.
Life inside the radio—
safe and secure, surreal
and silent at the command of my touch.

Fearful Flyer

He sits down next to me —
nervous, foreign, a nod hello.
Emboldened by Lorazepam and attempting
friendliness, I speak. Looking up
from his phone he mumbles something
about the ongoing trial, the witness-free
prosecution of a president. Odd.
What outcome does he want and why, and then what,
and must he stay poised over the cupped phone,
sneaking looks at it again and again?
The airport had been playing that old tune,
See something, say something again and again.
Older, well-dressed in slacks and sweater, he bows
his head and prays before takeoff.
He is flying from Florida to Baltimore to Florida.
Likely? He lives in California.
I follow a stewardess to the back of the plane,
explain that I am a fearful flyer and a little anxious
about my seatmate who is probably just fine.
Looking into her blue-eyed smile,
I see instead all the encapsulated innocence
that daily hurtles through the air above the earth.
I return to my seat, almost relieved, almost resigned.

Tanka

hot May day
at ground zero
seeking shade and rest
we can stand up
and walk away

Obama studiously
circles round the greys
annoyingly
reddening those who know
everything is black and white

as the season ripens
she returns to their bed
to close out the nights
lying sleepless
she shelters his weightless frame

Renaissance Institute

Not with the fear of the child
or the bored bravado of the teen
or the college students' credit count
do we seniors return to school in the fall,
some never having been willing to leave, some
filling hours, most finding something
of discovery, of youth in community, of purpose,
though age, too, quietly walks the shady halls,
stealthy companion
Books open to the loved familiar,
or brightly new worlds,
brush to canvas, ear to music, we continue
even as our cohorts fail and fall,
our faces turned to the temporary teacher,
seeking a little more wisdom
We study toward our final day
as if to pass a test

WALKING

Stranger with a cane
softly speaks of suicide
and of the life he found
in the Word. Swinging the stick,
he smiles as he turns toward home.

H_2O

One Summer Night at the Beach

Away from the bright city the sky
surrenders its secretive multitude —
the bashful, dimmer lights —
back-up armies in the distant
host of shining stars.

Gazing up, we wonder at stars' ages,
their number, posit possible planets,
imagine ancient times when we
first named them, first
realized that they steer our way.
We imagine their violent birthing,
violent dying, consider the time
we would use to reach the nearest star

and all the while the seaside breeze
caresses our clammy skin, brushes
our faces, dances with our hair,
as it is wont to do
then
fitfully attacks the folded sun
umbrella in the corner, persistent
in its irritated snap at the bundled
dress, in such protest that I turn,
finally, to acknowledge
its understandable scolding
of our inattention.

Sea Wind Musings

A rain filled weekend at the beach
requires a sense of humor
the *desired* water out of reach
A rain filled weekend at the beach
if nothing more will clearly teach
if family fun is merely rumor
A rain filled weekend at the beach
requires a sense of humor

Preservation Techniques

The beach has changed.
The gentle slope that met the wave
now steep, cliff-like in parts.
The water slaps
loud as a shot,
bubbles over the cliff
like a witch's untended cauldron,
slips over half the wide beach,
its towels, sandals, chairs, unsuspecting
bathers. All this due to efforts
to stop erosion. Efforts
that have also added danger
for the swimmer who does not know
the beginnings and endings of things.

The working sandpiper knows,
plays tag with the sea,
pursues the receding wake
only to allow the sea to chase him back,
scurries a step ahead of the wave
at his tail. He stops exactly
where the watery assault ends,
though each wave unique,
each pause as precise
as if he remembers what has never happened before.

THIS I SWEAR

The Skyliners

The lake is lovely;
man-made, two miles
long and just wide
enough that you would
try to swim across
if it were allowed.

Grassy slopes, dotted
with homes, yards
perfectly manicured,
buttoned with well-proportioned
trees appear as if someone
poked a finger into the middle
of a nice flat, planned landscape
to make a dent deep
enough to fill
with water for play.

The stillness beneath exquisite
Gainsborough clouds, is
disturbed only, but often,
by the roar of jet skis and boats
that course the lake's length
not quite constantly.

If you sit on your dock to
watch the sun set red
on the water, you might
see a wolf spider tread
the web being constructed
in air between two posts
by its odd, thin bodied, long-
legged cousin —
stilly waiting and patient.

At dark, water calmed,
stars, absent in the city,
assure you that they have not yet
vacated their allotted silent spots
so that you may settle on the porch
only to hear —
from three doors down —
Classic '50's Rock.
Last Date, Smoke Gets in Your Eyes,
There's a Moon Out Tonight,
Harbor Lights and more
fill all the night,
which, you learn, means
the owners are in their hot tub
and which, somehow, amazingly,
sounds perfect.

Loch Raven

When you crave ocean waves
but reservoir ripples
are your fate for the day
And your dog claims all trees
as he *flees* from the geese
And your husband's bad knees
slow your ragged retreat
the brief touch of water
a few feet of damp sand
somehow nearly suffice

Not Elizabeth Bishop's Fish

I too caught a fish.
We were both small, we were
young. He was silver,
no scars, no history written
on his scales,
no ocean, no lake, no boat—
just a stream somewhere.
My best friend's father, our escort,
our guide for this day, put the rod
in my hand, stood me on the bank
as we three streamed along the edge
waiting.
He must have tugged, I must have pulled,
reeled in the line.

I saw my fish with eyes at once as watery
as his were all at once dry.

Quickly rescued by our fisherman, we two
fled back to our separate worlds,
my last fish and I.

FAMILY

My Grandfather

Sits on a chair among nine of his siblings,
all old, all sun-touched in the shaded woods.
I never knew the others but he looks
out at me with a serenity
I almost remember, almost understood
as a young child.
All those faces, those arms, legs, bodies
long scattered into solitary graves.

They started our family reunion that now
stretches 100 years. This minute
I miss them, want to add my chair to theirs,
want to listen to their voices, their talk of England,
to the laughter that surely came out of such
a day, such a time.

I would not tell them stories of today,
of summer's end and the cold that hides
in the day's heat.
I would not disturb the quiet
that fills the picture,
as I cannot disturb the quiet
beneath his stone in the cemetery.

Faintly Found

She shuffles from place to place
looking for the day's belongings —
toothpaste, shoe, plate,
a button, her sleeve

Still hands quietly folded
soft words slip
from her lips — half thoughts
half sentences
Repeat

She holds her favorite
paperback open
as if to read
as if her fading eyes
do not deny the mysterious
print, the old plot

All our long distances silenced
My sister is losing her self
How gently you can brush
blush onto a familiar cheek

Janet

Florida tanned, dog in lap, peering out quizzically,
my sister looks at me as if she can still ask
how I managed to do whatever she now sees she
   might fix.
I chose this photo from all the rest.

My sister looks at me as if she can still ask,
though she cannot hear me or see me smile.
I chose this photo from all the rest
as she seems ever waiting for my voice, as I, for hers.

Though she cannot hear me or see me smile,
I can still manage to do whatever she might have
   seen fit to fix.
She is ever waiting for my voice, and I, for hers
Florida tanned, dog in lap, she peers out
   quizzically.

JANE

My sister asks for a poem
somewhere to hang
our hearts
because we are aging
into confidences
closer to endings
are our belated
beginnings

She asks for a poem
to hang from her heart
though it is so crowded
there and sentimentality
crowds the artful line.

So I say I cannot write on demand
though it is fear that I don't understand

Katy

Because she is young
the diagnosis strikes deep
into time, the brief and the long
her will propelling her on.

The diagnosis strikes deep
beyond the fair-haired family of four
her will propelling her on
to win before the battle begins.

Beyond the fair-haired family
into time, the brief and the long,
she means to win before the battle begins
because she is so young.

AN OLD PICTURE

Sits on my dresser in its original frame
A young girl poses to her right
Her head turns toward you
though her eyes evade your own
She seems to be about five years old

She looks much as I did at that age
The dark eyes those bangs
The short-cropped hair

Her smile is faint and if you cover her eyes
you are not sure her lips smile at all
If you cover her lips her eyes look wary
Already

Already not quite seeing you satisfactorily
Already looking askance
at her determined and measured life

SOMETIMES
for Debbie

if you wait long enough
another sister might pop
into your family tree
so that you finally have one
who knows, as you do,
that some rooms need be red,
some green, some Victorian,
that heaven is the sparkling
grace of a mountain stream
and you learn that your mother's life
was unusually sad

ONCOLOGY WAITING ROOM

Reading about centuries old church
in ancestral English village made
of pebble scraps and open
on Sundays

Scraps of conversation —
a woman vows never again
such treatment
another smiles back,
"you'll be fine, you're a survivor,"
returns to her magazine

My daughter texts from her exam
room about tomorrow's no more
cancer party, her 20th

Jane Austen bio on my lap
all sense and sensibility

Jennifer's Birthday, 2009

When we were camping in Colorado,
nestled into the Rocky Mountain Park,
when her sister was merely 5, and she
not yet born, a family from Iowa
in the site next to ours sang — together —
all day long
so that we sometimes felt trapped in
our tent by our embarrassment for
them and by our quiet giggling.

John Denver's songs of mountains and sunshine
and joy that had drawn us to this place,
filling our heads with anticipation
remained our private inspiration

So, last night, when a few of her friends gathered
at our house to help celebrate her 32nd
birthday, and her sister played Denver's piece
that gently croons;
"We want to call her Jennifer,"
you would not have thought that we three
would stand and hug her to us and sing to her
that song of long ago —
aloud, shamelessly, with no thought for others.

MOTHER OF THE BRIDE

Two different earrings, both pearl —
one stud, and one dangly. The mirror
does not tell me which is best with the dress
this wedding morning, so I consult
my husband. "The dangly one," he says.

We just have time to admire the bride, smile
with her smiles, pose for those pre-nuptial
family photos — a slight but strange floating
sensation carrying me along, bearing me
up the courthouse steps to where the groom,
very smiley too, waits with his family.

The ceremony clocks in at 2 minutes.
The two of them giggly, the bride quickly
trying to swallow a mint she has popped
seconds before the clerk finally flies in
to hurry them into marriage (after 11 years).
More photos.

Then countryside photos upon photos.
Dinner and photos — the two families bound by prints.

Such a simple wedding.
So easy to plan, so little room for mistakes,
so few people to witness.
I think I say only one silly thing,
and that to neither bride nor groom.

Finally, yet so soon, the farewells.
Then I am home, heels off,
feet up as I reach
to remove my earrings —
one stud, one dangly.

PROGRESSION

Excavation

Night
I remember crying in my uncle's arms
Noise of voices all around
Someone talking about the train
My mother was gone in the morning

My father colored with me after work —
big snowflakes made white against
Santa's red coat
Someone could happily climb down into such pictures
My father fed me tablespoons of pink medicine
through nights of illness, combed my hair,
whistled me home at dinnertime and dusk
My pony, he carried me round and round
the downstairs on hands and knees
He tiptoed into the kitchen with me
one Easter to discover
what all the chirpy noise was about
That was when people dyed
chicks blue and pink and green to match
the season, then sold them to parents
Those chicks disappeared one day
I think they died young

My Father's Visit

Short sleeved in Baltimore's sweet sticky heat,
your cancer still its own secret
you sit in my shady den,
look up at me, surprised
at the sight of your own arms—
skin crepey, withdrawing
from muscle, loose on bone,
proclaiming age.

"This is what happens," you say,
half unbelieving.
Speechless, I smile, shrug,
turn away.

What settles the business
between the living and the dead?

It is cold today.
The skin of my hands, loose.

MY TELLER OF TALES

When I learned you were dying
I mourned the coming silence
that would swallow your voice.

For all your fine stories,
I had yet to hear those
framing your youth
into the bones and blood
of my roots, naming me,
anchoring me in this world.
Had I ever asked?

At home, you bore our ministrations
along with your shame at needing them.
"So many hands and only one pair of socks,"
you sighed, helping us smile once more.

Remember this, then, I thought.

Then, wheeling you out of the hospital
into the late summer sun, whose tan
you still wore on your dear bald head,
we circled the helicopter pad and its red "X"
designation for emergency
take-offs and landings.

Enjoying the perfect day, you reminisced.

"When I was a boy," you said, "I
took my homing pigeons to school,
freed them to fly home where my mother
waited to note who flew straight,
who dawdled."

Our good-byes were brief—
you happily distracted by new visitors,
I, set to return so soon.

You promised, that last day,
to wait for me.
But you flew.

Experience

After my mother left
I was a child
playing cowgirl
in front of the TV westerns
I was already anticipating
my father's death
considering whether it would be best
if I were to die first, or if he should.

When he died, the unbearable grief
I had so long imagined lost much
to anger, to a feeling of the stupidity
of things — of his dying
hours before I got there —
of his dying.

I was surprised.

At the funeral home
I was curious to see, to touch
his body, empty and heavy
solid with preservatives

And I was sure, for the first time
however briefly, of survival
of the spirit — somewhere else —
for his was so obviously missing.

It was thrilling to consider.

The priest, my father's friend,
spoke of sin and Jesus, sin
and Jesus, and nothing
of my father
whose single soul
was far more vast
than that limited refrain.

I nearly cried out at the irrelevance
and glowered as he rattled
off the burial rites at the grave.

I have feared that I cannot
surrender correctly to grief
if I did not
for my father.
I fear I must be tested
until I get it right.

Man in Space

It begins with a beat
a little hip-hop smaller than a thought
disturbing no one, not even its source
Grows into an all-consuming idea
Finally claims for itself the light and air
and the things of this world

A boy, let us say, and we shall give him a good life
In sustenance and in loss something of his soul to be formed
We may say that he gives of that soul-filled self
at least as much as he takes in his time
and when we do, we may see that we are gifting
our own father with all he could have been

So that we grieve the lost good when he is gone
So that when we escape those gathered in mourning
and find ourselves alone under the sun
we cannot but imagine him spiraling up
into the fresh clear sky, smiling, disappearing
into the space where some say all things begin
and some say all things end

ENOUGH?

In lucid dreams, they say,
you receive your messages
from the newly dead
Conflicts are resolved
love affirmed
survival itself posited
bringing peace

So I wondered if my father
would come to me
to do that
this gentle man
who chose to express
life's joy and humor, who
neglected to address the rest

And he did come

As I ran to him in dream
weeping to find him
standing before me, he said merely,
"What?"
in that way he had
when he thought
you were unnecessarily worried
about one thing or another

CURRENTS

ANNIVERSARY

It was my birthday
I know where I was
when it was around noon in Dallas—
reborn into a new weeping world

I know where I was
in time's inefficient clock,
reborn into a weeping world
where the cogs slip unfixedly back

in time. Inefficient clock
For fifty years, a moment away as the limo turns
The cogs slip unfixedly back
to the sun, his smiles and the auburn hair

Fifty years. A moment away as the limo turns
to the sun, his smiles and the auburn hair
when it was around noon in Dallas
It was my birthday

NEWS SYNOPSIS

Owners of a nursing home in
New Orleans pleaded not
guilty of negligence in the
deaths of their patients
during Hurricane Katrina.
Safer to keep them
inside, with food and water
than to try to move them,
they claimed.
No one would have died
if the levees had not failed.

Factory orders were
down last month.

A Good Man Is Hard to Find

The pope has been gone a week
in which we have executed a prisoner
threatened Middle East refugees who are
not here yet
fought over giving poor women health care
built a brief audience with said pope
into a posited affirmation
of prejudice disguised as religion
fretted over conducting too weak
a war, left the homeless hungry
as they were
while we all calm down
from the excitement of entertaining
this man who speaks the old words
of love and peace to this
Christian Nation

An older woman-student
in a classroom tells the man
with the guns that she is sorry
for all he has suffered
That's not enough he says
and then he shoots her in the head

Ismene Speaks to Me After the Election, 2016

I fear I might become a passive stone that escapes in thinking instead of taking action.
                                    Cynthia Kittler,
                                    NYT, 11-13-16

My sister. My sister. We are not she.
It is I you know who inhabits your soul.
No matter. No matter.
You cannot dare to fly by reading a book.
You who crawl might yearn to be brave
wish you could save this world full of Hamlets
who merely break for the king. In order to be.
Cassandras warned and nothing has changed.
My star, Antigone,
whose hubris eternally chastens the state
yours merely human.
Your 21st century wasteland awaits
if promises hold. You say you are just one woman.
And like me, you simper and swear at the fates.

But I — I slept in the palace under his eye
the murderous noose just one way to die.

GEORGE FLOYD

My father, it is said, called for his mother
as he lay dying.
Men do. Women do.
No strange feat to relive the past
to seek the one who gave the life
that is leaving.
My father's death was private
though filled, no doubt, with pain and fear.

But what is it to call at the last
for your mother
that most personal summons
in a gasp before the world
as if calling to Earth Herself?

Too late, her fated children see.
Hot is our spring with rage and grief.
Silent is her witness.

WRITING ABOUT FOOD AFTER SEEING IMAGES FROM SOMALIA

What of the juicy joys of the berry
the vast fields of grain,
the sacrifice of the herds
for our better good,
the society of the *meal*?

What of the simple drop
of rain that does or does not fall?

Rerun 2020

A sonnet was a poem of love once.
Petrarch and Shakespeare evident pros
among a population of those
familiar enough at playing the dunce
who falls and loses or gains the world
for a time, though time the ultimate winner.
Is it love that has grown thinner,
or have the poets used up all the words that curled
around that pensive pen
so need to look to barer fare
to fill a dozen lines and two to spare?
The bleached heart of our leading man
pumps colorless and careless prose
icy as our solitude, narrow as our melting floes.

Reflections After an Election, 2020

The arc of justice is a man-made thing
elusive as wisdom, solid as air,
an anchor, a hope on a butterfly wing

that never soars but alights with a ring
of truth that to live is to dare.
The arc of justice is a man-made thing

whose ideal we posit from the man-made King
we deem sufficiently involved to care—
an anchor, a hope on a butterfly wing

lovely and fragile as the early spring
that hints at life, though is mostly bare.
The arc of justice is a man-made thing

of which the learned and well can sing
as though the lowliest have their share.
An anchor, a hope on a butterfly wing

too vague an aid for the man-made sting
of indifference. Mere see-saw progress where
the arc of justice is a man-made thing,
yet an anchor, a hope on a butterfly wing.

We Are the Experiment

A test to measure our mix of ingredients
to discover whether our molecules will bind
or if some will fall heavily, some rise,
some have the specific gravity to hold the middle.
Will the centrifuge of a spinning history separate
the whole into distinct parts, an emulsion
impossible
to blend?

It is hot this 4th of July,
our test tube clamped over the burner.
Will heat force color change, alter acidity,
harden or melt the substance of our being?
Or might the vehicle itself burst in the flame
like shattered glass
spilling the sizzling solution
into the fire or puddling inertly
until it is washed away, mere waste?

Can we discover, in time, a catalyst for stability?

WAR

Gettysburg, September 2014

1. I stand on Little Round Top,
   familiar site of bloody Civil War Battle.
   Two reenactors in Union Blue explain
   the old art of drawing, simultaneously,
   your gun and your sword, each housed
   in leather on opposite hips.
   They have serious affection for their roles.

2. A tourist in shorts and shades talks
   so long and enthusiastically about Viet Nam
   that the civil warriors are almost quieted.
   The men in blue manage to mention
   trench positions, which leads to agreement by all
   on those death-infested traps of WW I,
   which started one hundred years ago
   last month and which has not ended.

3. The quiet shade of the woods behind me
   absorbs the constant breeze that seems
   but sighs of ghosts.

4. Two other men stand gazing at battlefields below.
   The back of one's t-shirt reads something
   about destroying one's enemies and watching
   the lamentation of their women and children.
   He turns and I see that he is young,
   looks kind, is lightly bearded. The quote,
   I read, is from *Conan the Barbarian.*

5. The Pennsylvania Monument today
   shines like the Taj-Mahal, its bright white
   dome piercing the endless blue, its arches
   supported by walls of bronzed names
   of its silent dead. Amid its statued officers
   standing eternally at attention
   I find Abraham Lincoln.

6. Two nights ago, Barack Obama admitted
   that we must fight Isis.
   He has been so slow, so timid, some might say
   so womanly — almost as if he has lived battles,
   seen the tortured and dead, heard lamentations
   of women and children.
   As if he does not love war.
   And that does not matter.

Harriet Tubman

Rented out to put things right
for a spell, a list in your pocket
and trailing dust of those stars
that lit your way back home, in time.

What is it to be given to a world
that needs *you*, exactly?
What is it to be, disguised as you are
in the form of a helpless black slave girl,
a shape-shifting Odyssean woman—
sly player, victorious warrior for justice?

You might say you merely earned your peace.
Rested, ancient and shrunken,
your bright eyes still piercing the ether
until finally found again by the stars.

LANGUAGE LESSON

It is not yet winter
though the rose buds have frozen a deeper red
the mums' blooms are shrunken and dull
the anemones' stalks are barren brown

We work to clear out the dead
so that all is clean for the coming snow

It is not yet winter
but the dark web of noise
hurries that smothering blanket
that sour-lipped lie of White "Christianity"
History knows

Judas, I learn, is Latin for Jew
We shiver and claim that it is not yet winter
Though history knows

Possibilities

In fact and fiction that war has been onscreen
all my life. Old newsreels introducing cartoons
at the movies—before we knew to care, Hitler
making no secret of his psyche in miles of footage.
Images of the camps still shackle us to humanity's
sabotage of its own innocence.
So why, then, when I scout titles and plotlines
for entertaining escape, do I so often choose more
on that war?
In our stories our heroes are made; may win, may
hide behind a shrub, merely, and survive,
may strike in silence, like a Shoshone warrior,
and slit the throat of death itself,
may save their own lives
like some of the average people called to live
in that state of war learned to do.

The Photographer Returns

I have walked this ground.
It was shivering still from bombs'
assault, from the guns and cries
of those cowering in once
homes, barns, churches.
Long ago.
My job: To prove each splintered
timber's static bed beneath
the sun whose rays inhabit
once walled space, once paved
road, once roofed chapel.

To capture the living
The GI's, smiling, resting, marching,
holding children in their laps,
rifles in their arms, freedom
in their casual groupings,
power in their unstoppable tanks.
To freeze the woman in her stockings,
heels, her suit, her purse and hat
and the old man in baggy pants,
jacket and cap as they stand,
backs to us, among the shattered stones,
staring eternally at massive ruins.
They might be actors in a '40's movie,
characters so real as to be unreal.
All this in black and white.

Today I shoot again each landmark,
crossroad proven, steeple rebuilt,
mansion windowed and roofed,
quaint streets, road-side barns,
bright urban acres, all in
Kodachrome. Grass is green,
cars red or blue, parked quietly
near the once American-flagged
monument in the square,
the church a sunny yellow stucco.

The weary wads of troops are gone,
no man or woman stands and stares.
My camera cannot capture ghosts.
It is as if life has fled,
leaving me color merely.

I'll Be Seeing You

ached arcs of hope into air
that even Hitler breathed
and still that melody
haunts as if we are newly
separated from love
by his war
or are separated
from the Great American Song itself
and it is always war
or we are merely somehow alone

Gift

My Friend rushed the orchid to me
when her son left for Iraq, to thank me
in anticipation of the hours of listening, comforting
she might require
I feared I would kill such an exotic flower
That I might not succeed

My orchid did not bloom again for years
but lately it blossoms in late winter
looks out at the barren dogwoods as if to illustrate
for them how it is done — no fuss —
just a quiet surprise of white

Its petals tend to fall one day in May
after the garden has safely assumed its own colors

Again this wintry world needs comfort
Another burst of war
Another surprise of red
One orchid's bloom is a little thing
But it is doing all the good it can

September 11, 2011

Today my violet blooms,
a rare event, and an unfurling leaf
greens a long-browned stalk
of a plant I have neglected
to toss

too far away, too small
and too private a miracle
to heal anyone
even I want more

September 11, 2015

On the first anniversary
I took my dogs to the old trail
needing the sun and the trees and

their solitude. On another
I wrote of illogically blooming
house plants I had thought dormant

or dead until that greening morning.
Fourteen years of that day's replays
and I still wait for the dawning

in TV voices, the second
plane, the third, the fourth
disintegrating steel

and American naivete.
I cannot unwind today's wiser blue
sky or forget the cooling of distance.

OF TIME AND THE RIVER

Where I sit on a balcony
looking down at the Hudson
I see that the sun has caught a rippling
in what has been these few days
a calm surface flowing smoothly
south or quietly north
Now the southbound sparkles
with tiny fireworks
the northbound water
encircling its left flank
The current battle moves to a standstill
momentarily, as the sides appear
to be navigating a peace

I had hoped to catch this moment
to witness the ripple of time
as it brings all to a decision
temporarily
North joins the south's advance
for now, as the waters mingle
and they seek, together, the sea

MUSIC

Escape

I have been told I should listen
to more music and less news.
Take Russian, for instance.
Strings sweep like wind
across the steppes,
lift everything with them into the ether.
Piano keys prance, skip like sun
through village streets, scale marble steps
bubble into the night,
then fall,
softly plead the heart.
Note by single note they seek
and find the smooth response of flute or horn.
—always the strings sigh—
No borders, no armies, no little czars
never the dull ache
of the world's tired daily accounting.
Listen
till the melody is yours,
till you anticipate each note,
the laughter and tears of these old friends
who come to tell you what is true.

NOTES

I see them
seven small black notes
ascending and falling, over
and over again, in my mind
though their places on the scale
unknown to me, their sounds
mere echoes, remnants
of an afternoon's listening.

On my phone I find images
of the composer, Rachmaninoff —
youth to old age,
alone in sea-mist, or dancing,
laughing, playing with children —
action keeping company
with the soundtrack's music.

I cannot find in his face
his composition,
no hint of this century-old favorite concerto.

I have heard that music is about the silence
that surrounds the notes
that dot the lines on paper,
silence that fills the invisible air.
These vibrations that move me always
cannot reach the bones of the man,
cannot breach his eternal silence.

His gift given, his inevitable end
the still irony of immortality.

Chopin's Nocturne in E Flat Major

We are driving home from Buffalo
where my sister lives in her deep world
of confusion laughter and tears
I am a stranger to her
Irma is hitting Florida
where two of my sisters are
sheltering in place on opposite coasts
For diversion my husband
finds an old movie soundtrack,
The Eddy Duchin Story
Its theme piece, I remember,
determined the course of my music
professor's career and life
A moody Chopin steals you
away from other things
as it burrows into your soul,
engenders a melancholy so sweet that it is just,
beautifully, bearable

THE POETRY CHANGES

Take The King and I.
Aging both, our relationship
has changed. I mean yesterday
I did not wait for the sometimes
wonderful ruler's demise — on his chaise —
surrounded by his wives
and his one forbidden love,
though it was affecting,
or first lament both star-crossed couples'
melancholy notes.
No. I nearly wept at the upbeat widow Anna's
happy little heart singing of all the new
young lovers standing on that same old hill
where once she stood, the lucky one,
gazing at her own love
and at those same bright stars —
early, early in the musical plot
but late in time
for me to see for her
anything but winter
after that summer sky.

A Million to One

Once, a lifetime ago
I danced with a boy
—always and only—
to one song.

Too shy to speak,
we remained divided
by
all we did not know.
Yet, with the first notes
he appeared,
smoothly led me into
a dizzying world—
a 3-minute magical movement
that ended with each
final note.

Still, when I hear that song
I dance again with a boy
I never knew.

Dear Ludwig V. B.

Your metronome,
I learn, was off
You could not hear
You could not know
When your fate came
knocking
Did your fear thaw
like honey
slides — slow and sweet,
or did you bite it off —
a snake-fast strike?

Exit Interview:
Chairman of the Board

My life?
I gave it to 'em, sister.
The songs got it all
if it's feelings you're after.

This skinny kid sweetened their days
with a smile and a sigh
and a turn of a phrase.

Made 'em cry, you know,
and scream. Just me up there
singin' their dream.

Held my own with the cats,
the nights drinkin' Jack Daniels
till daylight crawled back.

Chicks dug the "ol' blues"
and I used 'em — like mink —
wrapped and warmed every one —
and I loved them, I think.

It's been a gas!

What? Would I take it all back?
The booze and the broads
and the dwindling pack?

Would you take, then, my voice?
Would you give me the choice
of silent obscurity?

Baby, I pass.

MY YARD

MASTERPIECE

This goldfinch sways on a long-stemmed flower
riding the breeze, careless of eyes, fleeting
gift to my garden, fleeting gift to me
in this day of cool quiet deepening sky.
Someone painted *The Goldfinch*, portrait to last
as long as eyes can see, museums stand.
Someone captured that *Goldfinch* in writing.
A double shot at immortality?

This squirrel, mouth full, stares at me and scolds
my usurpation of the porch. He is not rare
though he is memorably earnest—
graceful, industrious, self-important,
as immortal as your goldfinch, says he.

The Project

The steppingstones, warmed
in golden streaks and splotches
of ore—colors of Greece
or Rome, or Bath

lie on weedy grass before
the porch, spaced to step
you into the side garden—
shady beyond most plants' desires

yet happily dappled
by summer sun—
await planting of a sort.

The green must go.

Clover, viny runners,
bits of grass
sacrificed to stone

so that the gardener may
smile down upon what
she has sown.

LAMENT OF AN EMPTY NESTER

The house is still, now roofless,
mostly sideless, its dusty
delicacy wafted away
in the breeze or gently moved aside
because finally outgrown.
We unearthed, exactly one week ago,
a surprise of wriggling little grey-skinned
squiggles of something.
Quickly, we gathered them into a modicum
of their earlier home, though shallower,
more exposed to backyard dangers.
My daily (at least) examinations,
attempts at rebuilding, proved that mom
came at her allotted hours—dusk and dawn
For their bare skin furred, little ears
grew like Pinocchio's nose,
hind legs, like tiny kangaroos'.
All they needed, the last day I saw them,
was to open their eyes enough
to follow mom into the world
where she surely knows, after all her visits,
exactly where our lettuce leaves, tasty tulips
and baby zinnias grow.

Robin

Caught for who knows how long
between two panes of glass
in my closed garage,
a winter storm door and an old window
I had thought to sell to some artist
or craftsman on yard sale day
I assume he thought he saw a destination,
an escape forward or back —
beyond the mysterious barriers,
the walls he could not see
that thrust him
into terror and defeat
over and over
until he perished of trying
Did he not look right or left
to freedom?
He was beautiful
colors abnormally pale
an anomaly
a misfit

Nature's game

BOUNTY

Forget-me-nots have spread across my yard
from one small clump my friend once gave me.
Ignoring boundaries set with stones
or survey maps, they've blown and grown
into my neighbor's plot and slipped
around our houses with such ease,
leaving flowerless only shady spots,
that when they bloom we're looking over seas
of blue. Before they go, they seed
the next year's green, which winter cannot kill.
Sometimes I give some to a passerby
who stops to gaze, with warning
of their wanton ways, for there is
no empty sunny space they will not fill.

ONE SHATTERED BIRD'S EGG

Then two under the tree, fallen early,
before leaves can hide the nest,
years old, squirrel-built, not for rent.
Who dares such careless parenting?
A whole generation mislaid.

Before Waking

This now budding long-
stemmed lily slept one winter,
ignored spring, shunned summer's
sun, its luscious rain,
lamented not the fall's taking of its two
would-be companion leaves,
the ensuing indoor neglect,
surprises February
Solitary
Green lips slowly grinning
into an unfurling
unruly red mouth
trumpeting
itself

Natural Selection

These days of fires,
of floods and droughts,
of tornadoes, earthquakes
and spewing volcanoes
suggest a worthy concentration be spent
on the two babies in the nest
that has appeared
in the holly bush
by the kitchen door

October Surprise

Because the fox is strolling toward us
and he is slightly larger than my dog
I think it fine to go home
though the danger may lie more in my mind
He is slightly larger than my dog
this sly attacker looking pretty
Though the danger may lie more in my mind
it is time to act preventively
This sly attacker looks pretty
and though I wish it fine to stay home
it is time to act preventively
because the fox is strolling toward us

PEN TO PAPER

As I Was Going to St. Ives

I met a man with seven wives
and every wife had reasons six
to stick him with a legal fix
or with a knife or in a noose
His people let the scoundrel loose
to seek a dim-lit number eight
who'll sense she's met her perfect mate
For such is life for those who think
they'll mend a man who's on the blink

Sauce Robert

After *Sleeping Beauty, Part II*

A good cook can camouflage anything,
even if her boss is an ogress who desires
to serve her grandchildren at table.
(She must have read her Greeks)

Robert makes lamb seem boy, goat seem girl
all to suit the palate, please the unpleasant
queen who does not appreciate the shock
of his well-rested not yet bride, and the two
little proofs of their dalliance in tow.
Best to burn uninvited guests, put them

on ICE, then swallow or spit them back across
the threshold — if you are boss and have a taste
for treats and threats and the cooks are gone
and your kingdom is out of magic sauce.

Snow White

Lives with these 7
little men for who knows
how long
learning, learning
in that little house in the woods
yet still naïve enough — even
after Eve — to bite
the proffered apple
How fortunate that Disney finally
gifts the dwarfs with names
so that when The Prince kisses
White awake and into happiness
ever after
we know it's true
because she has mastered
all her man's sides; the Dopey
Grumpy, Sleepy and Bashful,
the Sneezy, Doc and Happy too

Thoughts Upon Reading a Victorian Ghost Story

Did ever the frail mistress
of a house, pale, and languid in grey
or in creamy negligee, lie abed
year by year tended by her faithful
maid, yearn for the affection
of her handsome jovial neighbor,
a bit wan himself,
only to finally fall,
failing, to the floor, faint
unto death, at the sudden ruddy
appearance of her wandering
whiskeyed husband?

What of muscle and bone?
What of mind, pressed not
with even the simplest
household chore?
What leaves her soft and still
waiting, saying
yes, yes to nothing?

ODE TO THE GREAT AMERICAN NOVEL

Absolam, Absolam

You waited for me all my life
though I refused you, frightened by *Faulkner*
scrawled across your face. Oh, I had flirted
with Fitzgerald, *Gatsby* eyeing me expectantly,
sure of my surrender to his name,
but not until I entered the dust mote, sun hot
space of your first page, encountered your brief
confession of all that you are—
those few words ribboned, danced, stretched
and bloodied through you until they explode
in a mosaic, cascade of the old South—
gentility that swallows facts, changes
their DNA, spits them back as brothers, sisters,
dynasty at war with its skin,
sowing the dragons' teeth we reap today,
all in lines so long and sweet,
am I lost, clinging to you as to my own dust.

CENTER STAGE

O, futile imperfection —
mere memory —
will not freeze for me
each infinite second
of immortal mortal beauty —
this Hamlet

Rosencrantz & Guildenstern Are Dead

Suspended. Upended.
Each intended fraction
of an action purposed
slipping into time and
out of mind. Concentration
seeping, dissipating
while voices of "important
parts," brief interludes
with kings, queens, princes troubled,
briefly recall to wispy facts
in their bare anteroom.
The more they speak
the less they know,
their wit tripping
into inevitable silence
while we stab and glance
at fleeting words merely,
seek logic, are left to simply wonder
if we too are but
the minor players of our own
five acts' fade to black.

Archetype

In comedy
the old man or the old woman
shuffles past the amazing
consequences of the action
the car on its nose
the plane in the chimney
the baby straddling the fleeing dog
merely helping to fill the screen
nearly silent as scenery
seldom really seeing
only seldom seen

Watching *Howard's End*

Her face of calm beauty
looks out the carriage
into her future, a widower
to wed, a home to run, a life.
This actress embodies the written
words of a long-ago author,
just one of England's many,
England just one land in this world
where men and women are born
to put pen to paper
in order to see, in order that we
may witness the conceivable.

A carriage carries a woman
perfectly made for her part.
A prince finds his will.
A miser gives, spirits reunite
before we must turn
from evident truth
to our common day.

CLOSING LINES

WALTZ

*For Sr. Maura Eichner, Poet
Professor at The College of Notre Dame of Maryland*

Her face in black and white
on the fly leaf is yet flush as life
though she has been gone these many years
and I, her student, have allowed
this collection *After Silence* to stand
quietly on my shelf for many years
She lives still, again, in these poems
not limited merely to the words
Full of breath and blood

Tall and straight, she seemed to glide
as if on a cloud, her stride so smooth
her dance with life not a tango of push and pull
not a simple two-step or frenetic fox trot,
but a waltz held lightly in her partner's arms
She moved in keys both major and minor
Her eyes turned to the other dancers
knowing them at once her companions
She spun from Poirot and Miss Marple
to seasons and suicide, nuns, students, saints and her God
She sang of Fitzgerald, Jacobson, O'Connor, poets and pets
as she took us all on her turn around the floor

Meditation

Moon, when you are full
and low, I look to you
for solace, for in your still,
round witness all have lived,
done their deeds, peered in awe
at your mastery over distant stars
as if in blessing of our brief span
and of our passing.

In the Deep Woods

The stricken tree may lean for years
on a neighbor or two before
finally hitting the ground
Years of silent and steadfast support —
silent but for windy creaks
leafy ruffles, and tree talk —
reassuring words that the one knows
it will live on in the lives it hosts
the others promising to always remember
to stand by the fallen forever
which in tree time
might be long enough indeed

Destiny

Every year marks more clearly her decline
I tried to ignore, then explain away, the loss
— her hovering neighbors —
less attentive than threatening
staid in their witness
as they creep into her air space
as if by chance
as if in innocence

Her limbs grow bare and splotchy
though her skirt still sways
green in the fall breeze
Her berries ripen toward red
buds patiently await the spring —
a bloom they will never see

Dear Dogwood

You knew I admired, loved you in all your seasons,
your final winter colder than metaphor.
I praised you on paper — a brief immortality
there lamented your slow dying
your growing number of barren limbs.
I grieved your final, perhaps merciful, execution.

Your shade garden, I planted to replace the moss
that replaced the grass due to your pleasing shade,
now too much in the sun.
That it survives, indeed thrives, seems insult
to your memory, your efforts, your purpose.

Dogwood, last summer you were a stump
slightly slanted floor for a tipsy bird bath
a decapitated centerpiece for the ever-taller hostas
that once merely accented your beauty.

So, Dogwood, what then of your little bent-twig
trunk that now stems quietly from your side
its impossible green leaves laughing up at me today?

POETRY IS

The beautiful stranger glimpsed
in passing or studied from afar
whose name you will never know
whose frame stamps its time
and space upon your mind
whose cheek-line could make you weep
for the very hollowness
of your empty hand
whom you know the world must love
and slay, mortality so loosely draped
upon such grace
whose glance if offered in dream
wakes you into your own
beating heart

ONE ABSOLUTELY LAST POEM

The Visitor

Sometimes a deadline is a helpful trick,
a play-date fit to rouse your muse who comes
skipping and swinging her bag of gorgeous gifts;
subject, mood, a perfect word you can't refuse.

Sometimes she'll make a beeline for the door
at demands for work, desert you at a thought
you struggle to expose, which neatly grows
smaller with each shriveling written word
until it flatlines on the barren page,
as quiet as an empty dancing floor
she'll see, perhaps, as an inviting stage.

About the Author

SUSAN MARSHALL studied poetry at the College of Notre Dame as a continuing education student in the English department. She earned her master's in liberal studies there and coordinates the poetry workshop of the Renaissance Institute at what is now Notre Dame of Maryland University.

She resides in Baltimore, Maryland, with her husband Robert. Two daughters, Tracy and Jennifer, also live in Baltimore.

www.ingramcontent.com/pod-product-compliance
Lightning Source LLC
Chambersburg PA
CBHW060605080526
44585CB00013B/691